When I spoke at my Aunt Nancy's memorial service in 2017, I said that I couldn't remember ever seeing her without a smile. I also mentioned that she always greeted me with the words, "Hey there, Shortie." (Currently, I am 6'4" tall and I've been taller than Nancy since I was around ten years old.) She was a pretty spectacular lady and every memory I have of seeing her is a good one.

Making this book gave me the opportunity to know Nancy much better than I had before. She was someone with deep thoughts and a caring heart. I loved reading a journal entry she wrote as a young woman in which she described her dreams of traveling, then later reading of all the amazing places she was able to see over the years. She got to go all around the world.

She documented her routine in detail when she was on these trips: finding an English newspaper to read with her morning coffee, collecting postcards from every giftshop to send back home and filling them out from her hotel room at the end of the day. She recorded her opinion of every meal, and the way each new hotel compared with her previous stays. And of course, she took photos of everything. I think she must have taken a photo of just about every church in Europe. Of the thousands of photographs I saw, relatively few include Nancy in them because she was always behind the camera.

In making this book, I was able to hold letters and cards from my family members who are no longer with us, some of whom I never even had the chance to meet. This process has been very special to me, and I hope the result is something equally special. These pages include a small portion of her photographs, words she wrote in her journals over the years and some of her amazing artwork. She was phenomenally talented and her paintings convey the wonderful beauty she saw in her life.

I hope seeing these things brings you joy, just as they have me while making this book. Thank you for taking the time to get to know My Aunt Nancy a little better.

Daniel Aartman
October 2023

September 20, 1964

Fog. It is so very foggy this evening; hasn't been like
this for quite some time. Fog always makes me want to think
back and remember, and then not remember anymore. Watching
the ocean will do that too. There is constant rhythm and
motion with them both. It is a great deal like "life."
There is a pattern in everything. You have only to find the
grooves and the right band, and hope that it is the right
kind of music. Fog has a rhythm. When it rolls it tumbles
right up to you and its pushing, silent-thud all but engulfs
its silence. I can remember best when I am surrounded by
this silence. The lulling of its steady pace reminds me
that all else is silence too, and there is no other noise
than its silent-thud of remembering.

September 21, 1964
Here at home, just above the door in the parlor in large
red letters reads a sign -EXIT-

Today I was thinking over all that one word does and can
mean. EXIT - Funny thing about that sign, it is a lot like
saying, "The End." There is no such thing. It is too final.
The whole idea reminds me of the warning over the portal of
Hades in the Divine Comedy, "Whoe to him who passes near..."

An exit sign is a reminder that everything is beginning,
is new once the portal is passed. We have only to cross
and a challenge opens, a beginning, a whole new genesis
and life is ours. If only we dare to "exit" and then
begin will it be ours.

The beginning is the most important part of the work.

Plato

September 23, 1964

In the evening it is quiet. At 9 o'clock in the convent it is very quiet. I am sitting here listening to the noisy lights of the city. They are glimmering loudly and I can't turn the volume down. They are staring me in the face and all they can say is that it is loud down there.

From my room I can see Sunset Boulevard. The lights are bright in incandescence as they tell of the noise. A man's raucous laughter at the night-club on the "Strip" shouts at me through the glare of neon. He is loud because he doesn't want to hear, to know that one more will hurt, and he is his own deadly weapon. I can't stand his loudness. Yet he needs help.

In the middle of town, near the Colliseum, at Santa Barbara and Vermont, there is a black man there on the corner. Another man is yelling at him -shouting, screeching, screaming. He's white, so he can yell and call him "Dog." The clamor makes the "White" more convinced... He's better; He's not black. This is the noise of the lights. They sparkle and I feel lonely, not because I'm not down there, but because I can't do anything. There is certain loneliness in helplessness. Their sparkling noise keeps telling me what is going on and I can't do anything.

People, real people are down there - everyday people. Some are shouting, some laughing, some crying and they all need God, even with their noise they still need God. Maybe there wouldn't be so much noise if they had God, and even a little love.

For context, the Civil Rights Act of 1964 was passed less than three months before Nancy wrote those words. The movement for racial equality was in full force in America, but it was little more than a dream to so many people.

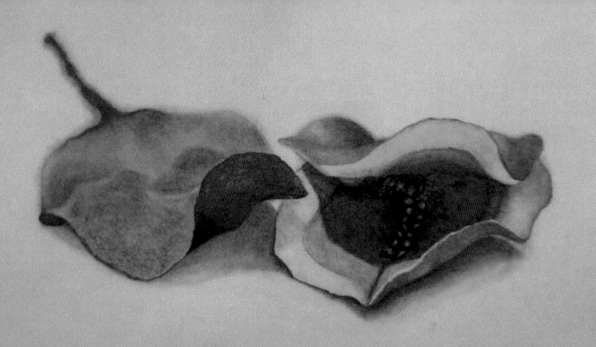

Munro

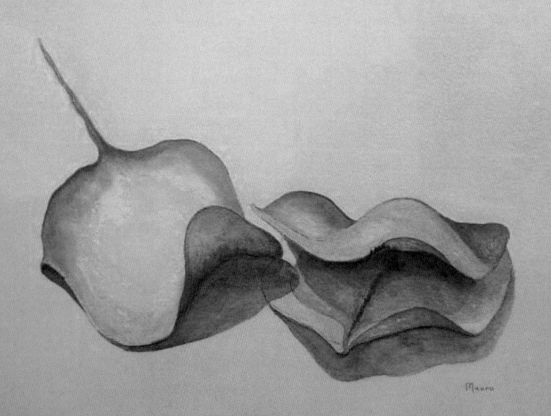

Munro

September 26, 1964

This has been a rather odd day. I have been thinking a lot about death, not so much with its actuality or realness, but the way people accept it in other.

Death is empty, dark, like a fog coming in off the coast. You know it is coming; you can see it roll and tumble toward you. It can't be pushed back and told "No, thank you."

I wish people only believed that and once believing it would welcome it for others. This resentful, "You can't have him" approach, or rather shunning, doesn't recognize the face of death as reality, as life.

The day a man dies is in reality his birth-day. The whole world should envy that man. Those that are left behind in the mire should rejoice that someone else, a saint, is going to be lending a hand from higher places.

I don't care much for saints who slept on nails and boards or pole-sat. I like the king I know; the kind that stayed here a while and knew me, sometimes just a short while, and right now are very close because they are apart. They loved death, even the young, for they knew that this was their way of saying "thank you," and our way of getting there.

September 28, 1964

Evil and fear may face the mind,
but can never hurt the heart if
there is love and undaunted faith.
I would rather face a grave than
lose freedom of heart and soul.
"The spirit of good that men crave,"
(<u>The Nobel Prize</u>, a poem by Boris
Pasternak) is the external freedom
of a man's heart. It courses through
veins and hearts that can never be
chained and manacled. Fear may come
- but only hate can destroy peace
and peace is just another word for
freedom of heart.

ancora imparo. I am still learning. Michelangelo

October 1, 1964

   In Mr. Frizzler's class today that frequent question,
"What is art?" was asked again. I don't think it ever
can or will be answered -- It is like happiness --
"Happiness is one thing to one person and something
else to another," as Peanuts would say. I think art is
like a person, -- and each person has so much to give
and be given if only he would be given the chance. Each
artist is completely different from every other one --
he is an individual. There may be a few set rules or
patterns that follow convention and should be followed
as regards taste and the like, but the individual should
never be subjugated to the ideas of another --

           the "good" should be sought after,
           not the patterns of someone else's thought.

October 2, 1964

People are good. They are
just trying to exist,
not much more than that.
People are good;
I must believe and
remember that.

assisi

Where spirit does not work with the hand there is no art. Leonardo da Vinci

We arrived in Italy on Tues. September 23 at Leonardo da Vinci airport (FCO) around 10:45 am — eventually we got through customs, got to the train station right at the exit of the airport and purchased tickets to Roma Termini and then from Roma Termini for Assisi. They €9 and €10 respectively. We arrived in Assisi around 2:00 ish in the afternoon and went straight to St Anthony's Guest House. We rested awhile and then went up to the Piazza San Rufino and ate a the Pizza Rustica. Sat for awhile and then came back to St Anthony's. Went to bed early and got up at 4:00 am to work on the...

ASSISI

October 3, 1964

"Do you ever cry?"
  I couldn't answer the question, at least really,
not because I didn't know or didn't want to say, but
because there just isn't any real answer yes or no.
It is because crying and tears are just as much a part
of living as breathing. I cry a lot, but my tears are
seldom seen. They are the quiet kind. They come when
someone says something sharp and just making fun or
during a sad movie. They come when someone has
"gone home" or when someone means to hurt. Some people
think that crying is silly. The odd part of it is that
I am glad I cry, not because it is "good" but because
I love. I love people and things, life and God. I
even love to cry-- it is like I said not because it
is good, but because I love.

Thanks be to God for simple things--for smiles, and baby hands and little children's loves.

I like small things like notes, when I'm down; a smile when everything is bad; a letter from sixth grade Bobby, or even someone telling me to stop feeling sorry for myself. They are little things, not even "worth" as much as a magnolia leaf turned brown in August or freshly cut lawn with a pup waddling across, but they are what makes life worth the stay and a God to be loved. I just wish I would stop and look at them more often. Maybe it is because I walk too fast with too large steps and don't really see the grass under my feet.

10/11/07 Valle San Martino

Giovanni & Lorenzo –
talked w. them in
front of their house –
nice people!

Valle San Martino

OCTOBER 9, 1964

Sometimes I think that God gave our minds to us just
that we might remember, that we might know and recall
and remember. I like to look back. Often it hurts or
just pricks but it is the way life was then. I remember
many things. I remember how Kathy and I would walk home
from school and watch the cars as they passed. We didn't
ever say too much as we counted the lines in the pavement
or stepped on magnolia leaves in front of the
Russell's house.

I remember these things, the small things that
happened because I loved them. They were all a part of
the ritual of life that occurred everyday for many years.

I don't see how some people can say there is monotony
or boredom in life. Every breathing, pulsating moment
is alive with something wonderful and good. People would
learn so much if they would only fix their open eyes on
the common, everyday living that goes on about them. I
learned more from stepping on dried magnolia leaves at
3:30 in the afternoon with Kathy, than all the world
of people's preaching could ever tell.

OCTOBER 11, 1964

Today was visiting day and Papa came as usual. The
thought of last visiting day keeps hitting me and I
think of Judy and Mama and Papa, and how Papa and I
talked about Judy last time. He almost cried and liked
going into the chapel. I only whish I could love like
he does.

Papa told me about Judy and how he watched her live
her last four months, knowing they would end. He talked
about her while he sat in the car and I could see the
tears in his eyes. I never saw Papa cry before. And he
has never had it easy. I love Papa.

the longer I live the more beautiful life becomes.

Frank Lloyd Wright

Finished my article and around noonish we went up to the large internal cafe the Piazza San Rufino — il Caffe Duomo — got it off to the Tidings. We walked a few meter and I came back to the Guest House to sleep — just sort of relaxed and didn't do much. Both of wine and FB and cookies for dinner. Thursday I worked on my sketchbook, put trying to get an internet, photographed the church of San Rufino, did the same in the

Piazza Commune and walked a bit came back and slept. A medieval painting going on in the Piazza Commune

Let the beauty we love be what we do. Rumi

ASSISI

St. Anthony Guest House

OCTOBER 11, 1964

Today was visiting day and Papa came as usual. The thought of last visiting day keeps hitting me and I think of Judy and Mama and Papa, and how Papa and I talked about Judy last time. He almost cried and liked going into the chapel. I only whish I could love like he does.

Papa told me about Judy and how he watched her live her last four months, knowing they would end. He talked about her while he sat in the car and I could see the tears in his eyes. I never saw Papa cry before. And he has never had it easy.

I love Papa.

OCTOBER 12, 1964

Life is meant to be lived and loved. There are hearts and souls to be loved -- real human beings all around us. They need us. I don't want to be way-out, apart from mankind; I want to walk along on the cobblestones of life and feel the un-smooth-ness of its path and the crevasses between the stones and the steps. God help me if I get lost.

never lose an opportunity of seeing anything that is beautiful;

for beauty is god's handwriting. Ralph Waldo Emerson

If you can dream you can create. John O'Donohue

OCTOBER 13, 1964

Kathy and I walked over the felty magnolia leaves
and listened to them crunch and watched the cones
scuttle across the pavement. The Russell's cocker,
Rusty, waddled down their newly-cut awn and his
splotchy-brown and white coat rustled with movement
of his old body.

Kathy's tired hands slipped out of mine, ruffling
around Rusty's collar and down the back of his ears.
Her five year old face repulsed in surprise as Rusty's
tongue swished over her blonde locks and wet her
right cheek. Kathy's fresh face showed the laughter
her eyes couldn't reflect-- she looked so tired and
the contrast between the dark sockets of her eyes and
the peachy complexion of her face made her a living
silhouette of what soon wouldn't be.

God loves children and God surely loves Kathy.

OCTOBER 17, 1964

I remember conversations, the people and places
and the souls in their eyes. The haltiness for words
or quick stutter of reluctance. I like to watch people
and think of why they say what they do-- and why they
laugh and smile or cry and think. Each person is so
different-- I only wish there was a way that their
hearts could be recorded and all that God wants to
say through them could be heard.

That is what I like about remembering-- it is the
people, their faces and their hearts. You can't really
forget a person.

Munro '09

OCTOBER 21, 1964

It is so good to feel at home-- and "Security is a
thumb and a blanket" as Charlie Brown would say--
Security is belonging somewhere.
I like to think of the "House of Studies Song."
Some of us were singing it at recreation today. It
gives me a warm feeling when I think of the words and
music. I think of the people I live with now and those
that were with us. I think of more than the words and
music; I think of what it means-- the desires that
impelled us and the sorrows that deflated us. Music and
words have a way of making people seem like they really
are-- all is seen in an instant and then lost
for a while.

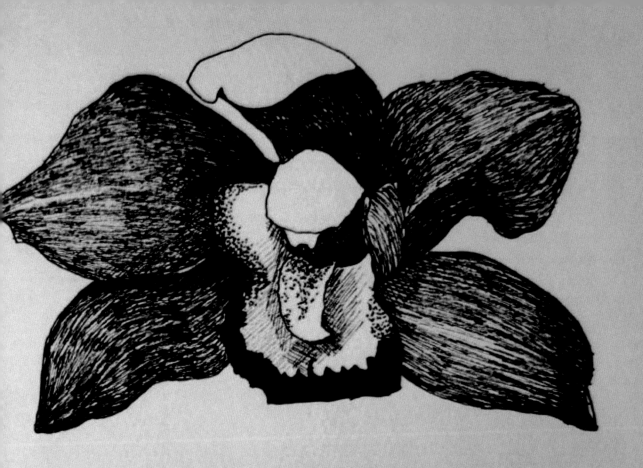

And the day came when the risk to remain tight in a bud
was more painful than the risk it took to blossom.
                                    Anais Nin

Each leaf in flowers. R. W. Emerson

The only journey is the one within. Rainier Maria Rilke

The flower is the poetry of reproduction.
It is an example of the eternal seductiveness of life.
                                    Jean Giraudoux

no pessimist ever discovered the secrets of the stars, or sailed to an
uncharted land, opened a new heaven to the human spirit. Helen Keller

OCTOBER 23, 1964

I love words-- I love them almost as much as people
and God. You can do almost anything with them. They can
be thrown against a wall and watched bounce back. You can
play with them.

I like them because I can make noises with them, make
rasping sounds, gentle ones and harsh ones. I can watch
them hit, and cry, and see them cover and shield or run
and hide. Each word has its own personality. Its own
peculiar way of looking at life and things and people.
They can be relied upon to go to just their right place
when told. They usually come at a call and very rarely
ever change without some notice. Even then they don't
hurt. With words I can describe sunsets and breezes. With
them I can watch a five-year-old clutch a toy dump truck
or listen to the crackle of peanut shells under the feet
of the person next to me, or see the tears in someone's
eyes well up and over the slits on the sides. Words put
in just the right order may make me laugh or cry or just
the point in between, the little ache.

Just as much as listening to words, it is just fun to
play with them. I like to play with words, see them form
groups, put bars between them making new words. I can
tell them what to do and they sometimes do it. They
listen when I speak in the quiet of my mind. They laugh
for me when I find it hard. They will cling to the paper
when I can't put them in the air or in people's ears.
They do for me what my voice cannot. I love words; I guess
I love them almost as much as people and God.

OCTOBER 27, 1964

That is real living and giving; when you can stop
complaining and look around and see what is going on
inside of other people-- see their tears and not preach
at the same time. It is really "being human" when a
person can see the whole world and its people and still
love it and them, Love is an activity, not the skilled
type, but a glancing around and seeing the dark roots
under the bleached white, and responding to the true
worth and beauty there-- not just the fancy and
superficial pettyness on top.

It is wonderful when people try to help others-- even
in just little things, and those are the best things--
To always be on the receiving end is a lonely, helpless
feeling.

OCTOBER 29,

1964

It is so bright out tonight and clear and I wonder
why people need so much light. There are neons,
billboards, and searchlights. I wonder why they need
it all. Maybe it is because people say all that is in
their hearts and souls at night, when it is peaceful
and dark. Maybe that is why there is so much light,
so that people won't think, or talk, saying what is
in their hearts. Lights are loud and shut out silence,
glaring in their glassiness. Light brightens and covers
with veneer what is on the inside.

I love the night. It is a tired time of the day and
yet it is the most beautiful. There seems to be no
hiding of reality in the night. God sort of puts a
blanket over everything and says that this is the way
He wants things to be. There is no arguing, just
acceptance, and life doesn't seem quite so bad afterall.

The way to know life is love many things. Vincent Van Gogh

OCTOBER 31, 1964

It is Halloween and not yet dark and there are no
trick or treaters up here. Halloween is a wonderful
thing; it's not just for little children, but for
youngsters. There is laughter, and fun and lots of
people, and dark. Halloween night is like a living
Grimm's fairy tale. One whole evening of
"Once upon a time…" I love fairy tales and make-believe.
I like to read "Winnie the Pooh" and listen to elves
sing "ah-oooo" in toy shoppes, and wish I had read and
heard them a few years ago. I guess that is one of the
reasons why I love children and youngsters. I envy them.
I envy their fun and laughter because I find it so hard
to have fun. I wish I could laugh, and see chimney
sweeps with black hats and coats, and hear Winnie thump
down the stairs behind Christopher. Bobby likes
"Winnie the Pooh" and fairy tales. He is getting sort
of old but he says he still likes them. We even talked
about them last Sunday. That is one of the reasons why
we get along so well.

Fairy tales are dream-like and I only wish I didn't
take life so seriously. Sometimes just to sit and have
fun, being rowdy-- "This is the stuff that dreams are
made of." It is laughter and fun and love. God made
laughter for man alone.

NOVEMBER 7, 1964

There are so many people in the world, and just that
many faces. I like to watch these different faces. Just
to sit and watch them walk by-- it isn't too hard to
read the lives written across the foreheads and in the
eyes. There are happy faces and sad ones-- but they are
all good faces.

NOVEMBER 11, 1964

Laughter is a wonderful thing. When things are hard,
it is good to laugh and forget for a few moments. God
must have made laughter with a special idea in mind.
It doesn't have to be wild or rowdy. It can be inside
as well as out. It really is just seeing the good and
enjoying it. It doesn't even have to be funny. I do
love laughter and it is always easier to appreciate
something when you don't have it as often as others do.

NOVEMBER 12, 1964

I like to doodle. Many people seem to think it is a
waste-- a uselessness. I think that sometimes it is
far better to keep the hands busy than not at all. Hands
are creative things and like the mind shouldn't be idle,
loose not caged in by patterns not strict ideas. There
is a potential for hands, even if only for doodling. They
can mould, form, create, even break. Hands can talk and
speak often far more eloquently than many words. Often
when I can't communicate it is my hands that speak for
me. Hands have their best power in this creation. Thoughts
can flow through fingers; into clay, onto paper and even
sketching doodles. The hands make new, real and lively
patterns-- something just a little different from anything
before or to come. They are alive with reality and
imagination and realness. And best of all after forming
thoughts with my hands I like to keep them busy doodling--
moving. It is relaxing and just interesting to see the
lines criss-cross in and out, dark and light, and know
that it all is something real, even if just that I want
to keep moving.

Art is the proper task of life.

Nietzsche

never pray in a room without windows

The Talmud

NOVEMBER 13, 1964

From my window I can see the hills behind Mr.
Campbell's ranch and the road that runs over it up
to "Everest." I ove to look at hills and mountains and
roads, and I remember what someone once said, that she
would like to just take a road and keep going and not
stop, and see everything on that road.

Sometimes it seems a wonderful thing just to follow
a road. But I guess we really are doing that every day.
Life is a road, and a person only stops once. There is
so much to be seen on that road, not just mountains and
hills-- but seas-- rumbling, rolling, and calms too.
There are sunsets and new mornings and colds and warms.
There is rain-- the salty and the fresh-- and there
is sunshine. It is all on the raod. Sometimes we get
lost in the snow and the rain and forget that there
is a thaw and a spring, a genesis and life. There is
always a spring as well as a fall. It is just when the
leaves are brown and down that we forget there will
be a green and a newness. It is all the cycle of life
and living on the road. It winds round and round in
cycles and the dizziness from the roundness makes the
swirl hide, and in whirling we just sometimes forget
the summer and stop at the end of the road.

It is at the edge of the
petal that love waits.
                    Wm. Carlos Wms.

achieve your own beauty
as the flowers do. DH Lawrence

DECEMBER 2, 1964

   Perhaps this is indicative of a certain oddness
but today I was thinking of lions. Now possibly this
is a very weird subject to occupy a person's mind, but
I was thinking that they are the grandest animals alive.
I remember when I took some pictures of a couple of
lions a few years ago. I thought then that they were
the most (to use an odd and trite expression) majestic
and proudest animal in the world. I used to check out
Osa Johnson's <u>I MARRIED ADVENTURE</u> at least once
every other month when I was in the
sixth and seventh grades. I would read and leaf through
the leopard-spotted covered book and think that
someday I too would go to Africa and shoot animals,
especially lions, with a camera. In my young
unrealistic mind I pictured the glories of seeing
and experiencing these "Kings of the Jungle."
Well, anyway, I still admire and love these animals.
There is something very captivating in the way they
move and take possession of the situation. Although
I do admire them I think that perhaps they are just
to be admired. And I will stay here and think of them.
Africa is too far away.

 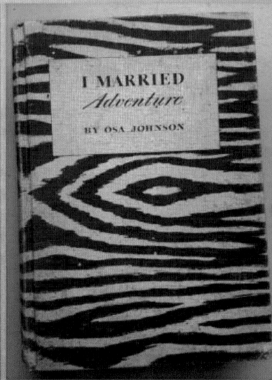

Munro

December 10, 1964

   Outside the community room window there is a beautiful
full red rose. It looks like a beaconing roundness in the
green. I like roses almost as much as carnations and
marigolds. They show beautifully the exquisite particularness
of God in creation. Everyhing has its own individual character
and identity-- like people.
   I don't know by name too many of the trees and birds and
flowers, but the ones that grow around here outside are
particularly individualistic. There are the tall, stern
junipers as contrasted with the lumbering pines across the
road. There are the perfectly round and formed roses and
the sometimes helter-skelter daisy. And each in its own way
simply or profoundly reflects itself and God. And I sometimes
think that perhaps the more simple things are the more
profoundly they do reflect God, the King of all creation.

You don't have to be tall to see the moon. *African Proverb*

DECEMBER 18, 1964

The dark cloudy sky looks like an upside-down ocean today. It seems so flat and silky like Grandma's old down-feather quilt and the junipers below our Lady's statue look like green spires ready to touch heaven and that bird on top of Mary's head seems to be daring the wind to knock it off.

I really like the view from the community room. I wish it would rain and be cold. Everything looks better and happier when it is wet because there will always be the sunshine and a new freshness after the rains. Damp things seem so close-- especially after the rains. Everything seems close now-- but it would all be so much closer if it would only hurry up and rain.

JANUARY 6, 1965

This afternoon after class I went up to the roof.
I stood for awhile and thought and watched. The clouds
were a beautiful white blanket over the ocean. And two
blue jays flew below and across the garden to the other
side of Chalon. I never noticed the way blue jays fly
before. Their wings are first out when gliding, then
they pull them back for more thrust, and then they
begin their glide again. It is a beautiful sight with
their wings extended and expanded at full width. They
are beautiful looking birds-- too bad they are so mean.

I saw many things from the
roof-- the various shades of
red-brown in the leaves of the
trees below, the helter-
skelter pine across the road
and the craves in the
pavement tarred over.

I like to look at things.

JANUARY 7, 1965

This morning I was looking out the window of Rm. 104
during class and the clouds looked like climbing
snowballs going up the side of the hills. They were
rolling, tumbling in tufts and seemed to be trying to
hide the hills in their running whiteness. It rained
last night and I am glad because there is a newness
in the air and sometimes that is what is needed to breed
hope in light of sunshine. Sometimes when there is the
electricity of tension and worry and anxiety in the
people and things about us we need the dampness of rain
and tears to ease the strain. And I guess there was a
great need for the dampness to put new light on things.

From Nancy's Sister Elaine:

It was the 4th of July. Nancy and I were staying in Mexico City and she had the idea to go to the airport and find the cheapest place we could fly to... just because. We booked a round-trip to Acapulco. We landed and Nancy insisted on buying a dress from this shop. It cost her less than five dollars and it was this pretty periwinkle blue color. We seemed to be the only Americans in the city, but they did have a huge 4th of July Celebration. We were dancing and drinking and of course it was quite humid in that part of the world in July.

By the end of the night, we went back to our hotel. Nancy went into the restroom and I heard her burst out laughing. Every part of her skin that the dress had covered was dyed blue and the rest of her was sunburned. She came out singing Ray Charles' "AM I BLUE?" It was unbelievably funny.

Nancy with her Neice Shelly and her Nephew John (No longer a newborn) at her Silver Jubilee in 1987, celebrating her 25th Anniversary as a nun.

Dear Aunt Nancy,   May 31, 1964
   How does it feel to be an aunt for the very first time? As you can probably tell by the picture, he's waving at you. He's such a sweet little thing and doesn't hardly make a fuss at all. They brought him into me for the first time last night.
   You'll have to excuse my writing but I am laying down in bed.
   Little John's hair is sort of reddish-blond and he's not at all red like some babies. I just love him to pieces.
   I'll write more after I get home. I get to leave tomorrow.

                                   Love,
                                   Kathy

May 31, 1964 .

Dear Aunt Nancy,

How does it feel to be an aunt for the very first time? As you can probably tell by the picture, he's waving at you. He's such a sweet little thing and doesn't hardly make a fuss at all. They brought him into me for the first time last night.

You'll have to excuse my writing but I'm laying down on bed

Little John's hair is sort of reddish-blond and he's not at all red like some babies. I just love him to pieces.

I'll write more after I get home. I get to leave tomorrow

Love,
Kathy

3/3   Sister Nancy Munro 1972

9:00pm
Thursday Night

P.S. Send Soon

Dear Nancy,
  I am watching BEWITCHED on Channel 13. Have you ever seen it before? Dick York is a father of a baby and His wife is a witch. Her husband forbids her to use witch craft. Endora is the name of wife's Mother of Dick York.
  Mom went down to Hales with Grandma. Grandma got two or three dresses for the trip down to L.A. We are looking forward to see you. Are you looking forward to see us? Maybe I can go fishing in the boat in L.A. Harbor. Last time I went fishing it was... in the Harbor. I didn't catch a fish.
  I am real proud of you and Mom is too. I hope you are doing real well. Do you like the parish you teach at? Do you like the Fourth Grade? Is it hard for you?
  Mom is knitting in the den. Have you ever knitted before? I have and I don't like it. Knitting is not such a hard deal.
  Elaine and I are watching Mona McCluskey. Have you ever seen it before? Starring... Juliet Prowse.
  Well, I got to get this letter in the mail. We will be seeing you.
x x x x x x x x x x x x x
o oo oo o o oo o o oo

Love and Prayers, Sam

This letter was written by My Uncle Bob, Nancy's younger brother. I learned that Sam was a nickname their family used when they were growing up.

Nancy with her Siblings Bob and Elaine
at her 50th Jubilee, March 2012

Nancy, Elaine, Bob, Kathy and Cathy from a celebration likely mid 1990s.

6:55 P.m.

Dear Nancy   November 19, 1965

I am watching the news but I just moved the channel and now I am on ten. Lawman has just ended next will be The Rifleman. that is a good program. I hope it is about a murder. they are always the best, well it is a murder. do you remeber it? I do.

it rained here today. last night the rains were just pouring down and our drive way was flooded even the patio, the people next door have there drive way flooded to. it so post to rain tonight and tomorrow. do you think so?

George is here in sacarmento, do you know that George has a Whip lash in his neck? He just went over his friends house. he painted his car white because of a sand storm in Vegas.

Mom is sew in th dinning Room. she is making me some Pajamas
Well My letter Must end.

X Xx X X X x x X X X x x x Love
X xX X X X X X X X X x x X
o o o o o o o o o o o o o Sam.
o o o o o o o o o o o o o o

6:55pm
November
19, 1965

Dear Nancy,
  I am watching the news but I just moved the channel and now I am on ten. Lawman just ended. Next will be The Rifleman. That is a good program. I hope it is about a murder. They are always the best. Well it is a murder. Do you remember it? I do.
  It rained here today. Last night the rains were just poutinng down and our drive was very flooded, even the patio. The people next door have their driveway flooded too. It's supposed to rain tonight and tomorrow. Do you think so?
  George is here in Sacrament. Do you know that George has a whiplash in his neck? He just went over to his friend's house. He painted his car white because of sandstorms in Vegas.
  Mom is sewing in the dining room. She's making me some pajamas.
  Well, My Letter Must End.
                                        Love, Sam

Nancy, Bob, Elaine and Kathy
with their Mother Gertrude

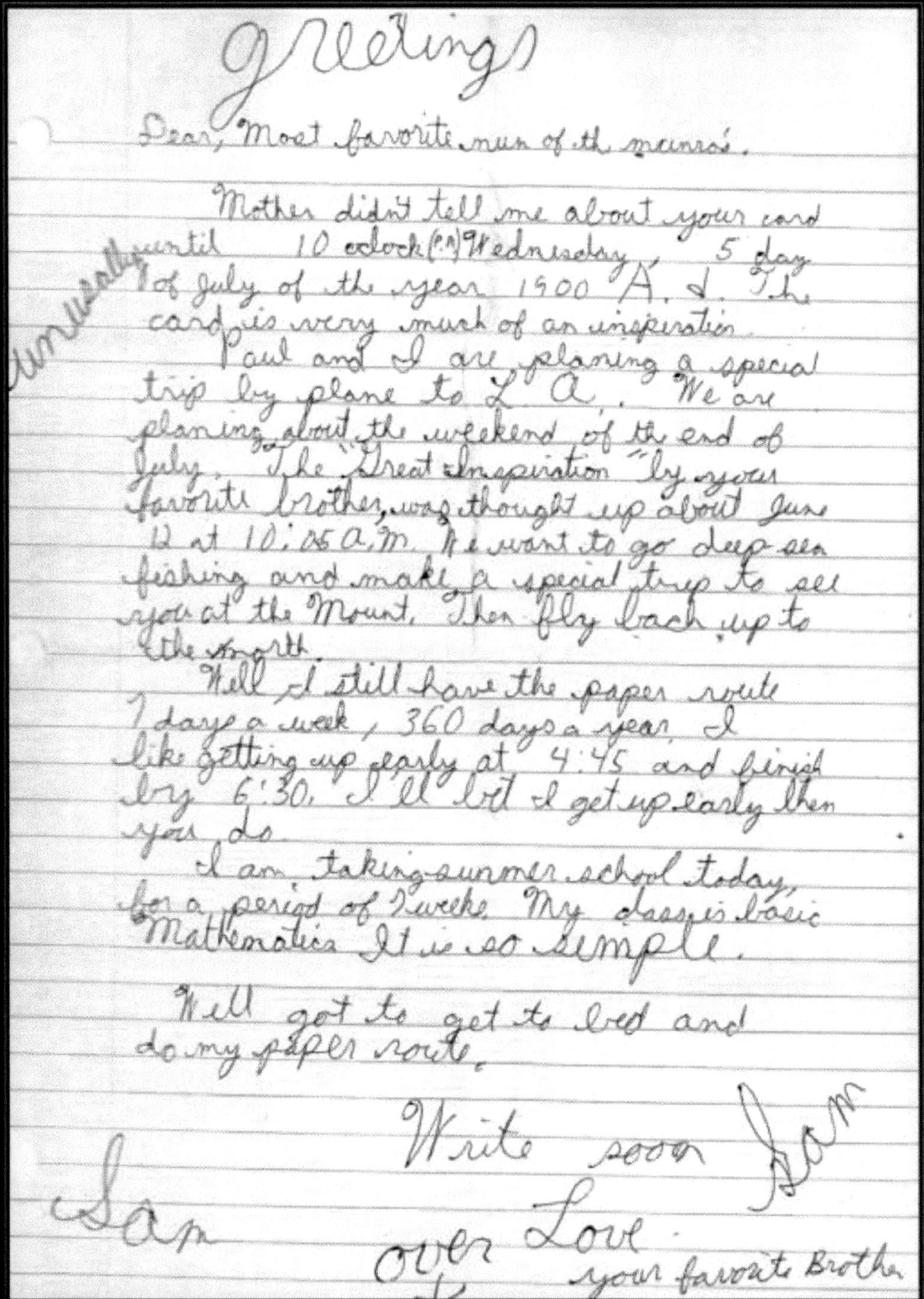

Greetings

Dear Most Favorite Nun of the Munro's

Mother didn't tell me about your card until 10 O'clock pm Wednesday 5 day of July of the year 1900 AD The card is very much of an inspiration.

Paul and I are planning a special trip by plane to LA. We are planning about the weekend of the end of July. The "Great Inspiration" by your favorite brother was thought up about June 12 at 10:05am. We want to go deep sea fishing and make a special trip to see you at the Mount. Then fly back up to the north.

Well, I still have the paper route 7 days a week, 360 days a year. I like getting up at 4:45 and finishing by 6:30. I'll bet I get up earlier than you do.

I am taking summer school today, for a period of 7 weeks. My class is basic Mathematics. It is so simple.

Well, got to get to bed and do my paper route.

Write soon,
Love Your
Favorite Brother

Sam

Greetings
Dear, Most favorite nun of the munro's.
Mother didn't tell me about your card until 10 oclock (P.M) Wednesday, 5 day of July of the year 1900 A. D. The card is very much of an inspiration.
Paul and I are planing a special trip by plane to L A. We are planing about the weekend of the end of July. The "Great Inspiration" by your favorite brother, was thought up about June 12 at 10:05 A.M. We want to go deep sea fishing and make a special trip to see you at the Mount. Then fly back up to the north.
Well I still have the paper route 7 days a week, 360 days a year. I like getting up early at 4:45 and finish by 6:30. I'll bet I get up early then you do.
I am taking summer school today, for a period of 7 weeks. My class is basic Mathematics. It is so simple.
Well got to get to bed and do my paper route.
Write soon
Love
your favorite Brother
Sam
Sam
over

Bagnaio and Villa Lante

Art is one of those things we simply must do so that our

spirit may continue to grow.

Dear Mother and Daddy

this little letter is to Wish you a very happy Christmas Morning. my first prayers will be for you. my dear parents I love you very much and I will

always try to be a good girl

Dear Mother and Daddy
This little letter is to Wish you a very happy Christmas Morning. My first prayer will be for you.
My dear parents, I love you very much and I will always try to be a good girl.

For me the journey that is life must have begun anew in Italy.

Since somehow God must have planned that I would visit Italy these last three times....I have been able to savor the sights and smells, watched the friendly faces and heated conversations, walked the many winding streets and interminable stairs, seen cathedrals that have lasted through centuries and even more beautiful tiny chapels and shrines--all monuments to a deep faith and profound sense of the sacred. In Italy there is a yearning for peace and sense of the place of the country in the global community. May I continue to be able to travel even more in this beautiful land.

Nancy loved to find ways to present her photos, whether in frames or memory books which she frequently gave to our family members as gifts. The words above are on the first page in a memory book she made after a trip in 2009.

harni

Ghirlandaio's "Coronation of the Virgin" hangs in the museum in Narni. The special exhibit was closed but a young lady working in the museum and unlocked the exhibit, put on music, brought us chairs and turned the lighting on the painting and pointed out the MAGNIFICENT painting--!!

Friday SEPTEMBER 14, 1979

   We motored down the Autobahn through the lovely
German countryside- trim fields, fat livestock and
the millions of trees alongside the road. Passed by
many small villages. It seems there is a flower box
at every window of every German house.

Thursday OCTOBER 4, 1979

   We stopped at the castle on the edge of Loch Ness
to take some pictures.
                The "monster" did not make an appearance.
   We made it on to Dingwall- Inquiries about my
grandfather got me nothing but I found my own name
many times in the little museum there. It seems I am
the namesake of some politicians and military men.

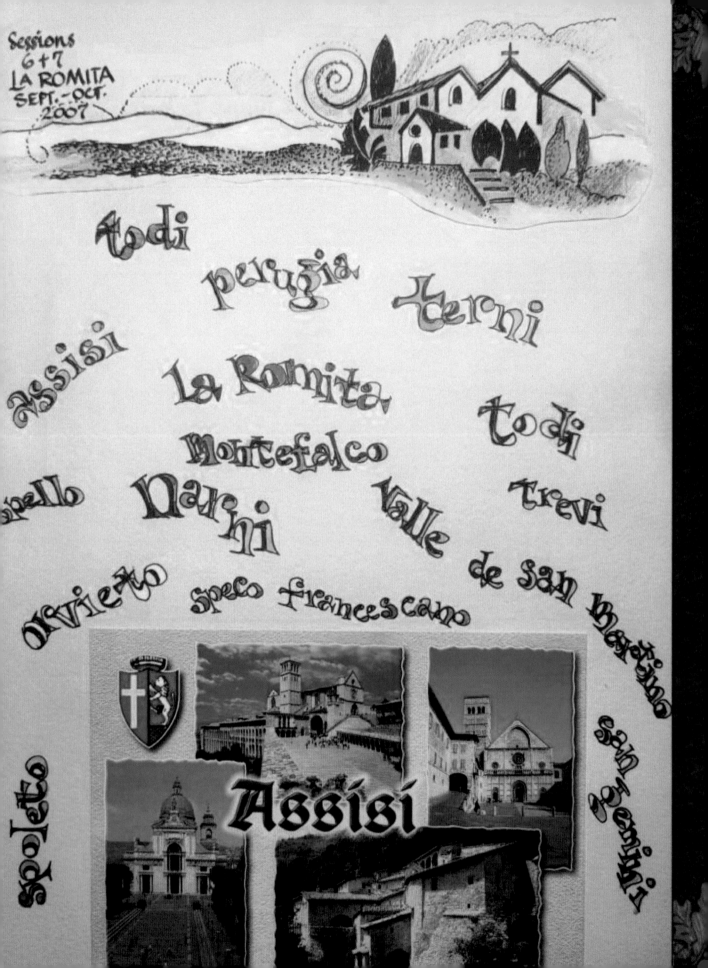

Sessions
6 + 7
LA ROMITA
SEPT.-OCT.
2007

todi

perugia

terni

assisi

La Romita

todi

Montefalco

pello

Narni

Valle

Trevi

de san martino

orvieto

speco francescano

spoleto

Assisi

san gemini

Thursday JUNE 4, 1981

Got to LAX early and enjoyed some pie and coffee before
we took off. Out plane, a huge 747, and as I write this
we have reached a cruising altitude of 29,000 feet- all
300 tons of plane and people. Because of the fuel
expended our pilot tells us the plane loses weight at the
rate of ten tons an hour - so the father we go -
the faster and higher.

Friday JUNE 5, 1981

Nancy and Jeanne (The other women on the trip) were
both able to sleep on the plane, but I could not. I watched
the approach of dawn from the plane window for we were
flying into the sunrise. At the end of a full day, we went
to bed pooped - but feeling pretty good about it.

Saturday JUNE 6, 1981

Traveling around London. There are bobbys everywhere
because of threats of violence by the Irish Extremists.
Even Downing Street was barricaded - so we caught a
double-deck bus back to the hotel. What a view it is from
the top of the bus - that was fun.

Context: earlier that year Bobby Sands, member of the Provisional
Irish Republican Army (IRA) was imprisoned and elected as the youngest
Member of the United Kingdom Parliament. He led a famous hunger
strike for the cause of prison treatment reform and died of starvation
exactly one month before Nancy visited the UK. Response to his death
was seen around the world.

Wednesday JUNE 10, 1981

We took off (from our hotel in Marche, Belgium) like a
pack of jet-setters to have breakfast in Belgium, lunch
in France and dinner in Switzerland. There has been the
appearance of prosperity everywhere and France seems like
one big vegetable garden. The row crops were precise -
the grain fields rippled in the breeze - the fruit trees
budden or laden and the cattle fat. And then there were
the poppies.

Thursday JUNE 11, 1981

Now the girls have tripped off in search of bargains
in the many shops. I am comfortably ensconced in a warm
sunny seat alongside this lovely lake (Lake Lucerne in
Switzerland) - reading my paper- scribbling from time
to time - thoroughly at peace with the world. I probably
will regret leaving when it is time to go back to the
coach. This is a pretty, bustling place, full of
enterprising merchants. Prices are sky high but then so
are our spirits.

Sunday JUNE 14, 1981

(In Italy)
The coach took up to the ancient Roman Forum - the
Colisseum - the Palatine Hills - the Piazza Venezia and
to the Pantheon - most remarkable of any building from
antiquity that I have seen. Then, as a surprise, we were
informed the Pope (John Paul II) would give his blessing
from the apartment window at noon. He gave a brief talk -
it was a thrill to see and hear him. The square filled
with countless thousands of people.

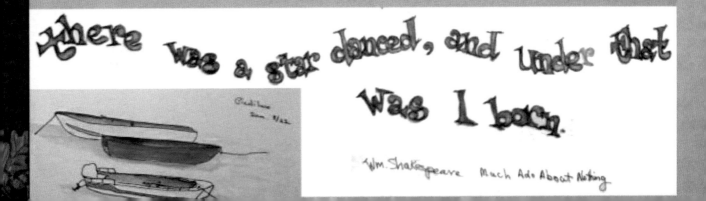

there was a star danced, and under that was I born.

Wm. Shakespeare   Much Ado About Nothing

Munro

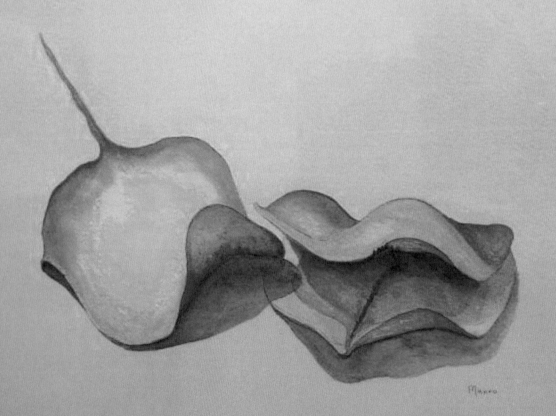

Munro

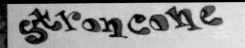

Stroncone

Life isn't long enough for love and art.

W. Somerset Maughan

Thursday JUNE 18, 1981

(In Lyon, France)
   The bottle of wine that the girls had with their dinner
last night must have been grand stuff. They are still
talking about it and I noticed their eyes were like
stars when they came stumbling out of the restaurant.

Sunday JUNE 28, 1981

(Leaving Loch Lynn, Scotland)
   On the drive out, Nancy spotted a Scotsman all decked
out in his kilts and playing his bagpipes on a lonely
and unlikely stretch of road. She thought that was
"pretty good." So it was one of several stops for picture
taking. For raising that kind of din on a Sabbath morn
I am convinced the scoundrel should be hung. Oh yes -
the lad had the presence of mind to provide an offering
box close at hand - he is church-trained, obviously. This
is wild and rugged country - but beautiful.

Wednesday JULY 1, 1981

(Oxford, England.)
   This is Lady Di's birthday - her 20th - and the papers
are full of the plans for a celebration. I wish we could
be here on the 29th - that is Nancy's birthday and the
date for the royal wedding.

"It is the 25th of December," said the Historian,
  "A date established by the Council of Nicea
    To appropriately observe Christ's Birthday
    In conjunction with the Roman feast day of
      the Lupercalia."
"It is the celebration of Christ's Birthday in the
    hearts of men," answered the Preachers,
      Priests and Congregations.
"It is the Christmas Tree and Santa Claus and toys
    and presents," said the Little Child.
"It is the most profitable motivation for merchan-
    dising goods of the whole year," replied the
      Business Man.
"It is the most beautiful observance of our religious
    tradition," answered the Artist.
"It is that day," said the Sociologist, "when men
    most wish each other Peace and Goodwill."
"It is that time," replied the Psychologist,
  "When people most rationalize their feelings
      of guilt by diversion, feasting, revelry and
        exchanging gifts."

But the Lonely Man was confused, and he went
Apart from the World and knelt and prayed:
  "Tell me, Holy Spirit, what is Christmas?"
Then fell upon his troubled Soul a peaceful calm
    so sweet and still;
And a loving Voice within him answered, saying,

  "Christmas is that moment
  when you kneel to seek my will."

To nancy
  with love,
  Uncle Charles

Christmas, 1970

Dear Elaine,

Well, Happy Valentine's Day AND Surgery Day!!!!

The other day I went with a friend to the Gene Autry Museum—a really nice place for art lovers. He had quite a collection of Western Art & invested his money well. Before leaving I went into their museum store and got this little book. It reminded me of you — not so much for what it says but more the concept of cow gal saddle pals.

Heal well. Rest. And please don't overdo the foot. OK? I care, and none of us is as young as we were once upon a time...

Good luck on the surgery and please be good to you!!!

Love you,
Nancy

Bob, Kathy, Elaine, Nancy, Gertrude and her boyfriend Ted.

Nancy with her Grandmother Mina

poetry of the earth is never dead.

John Keats

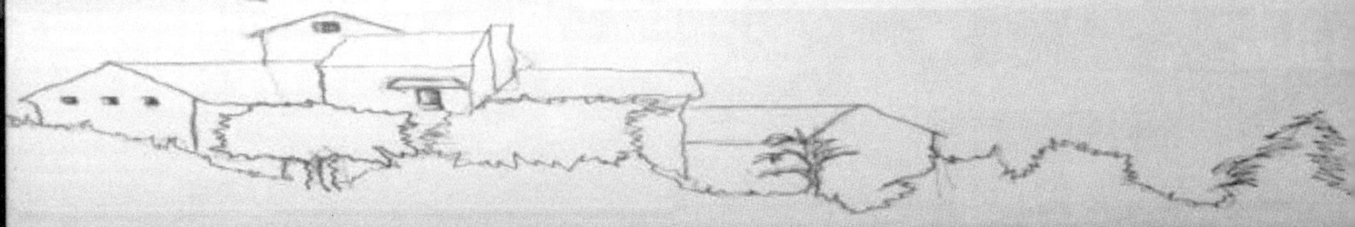

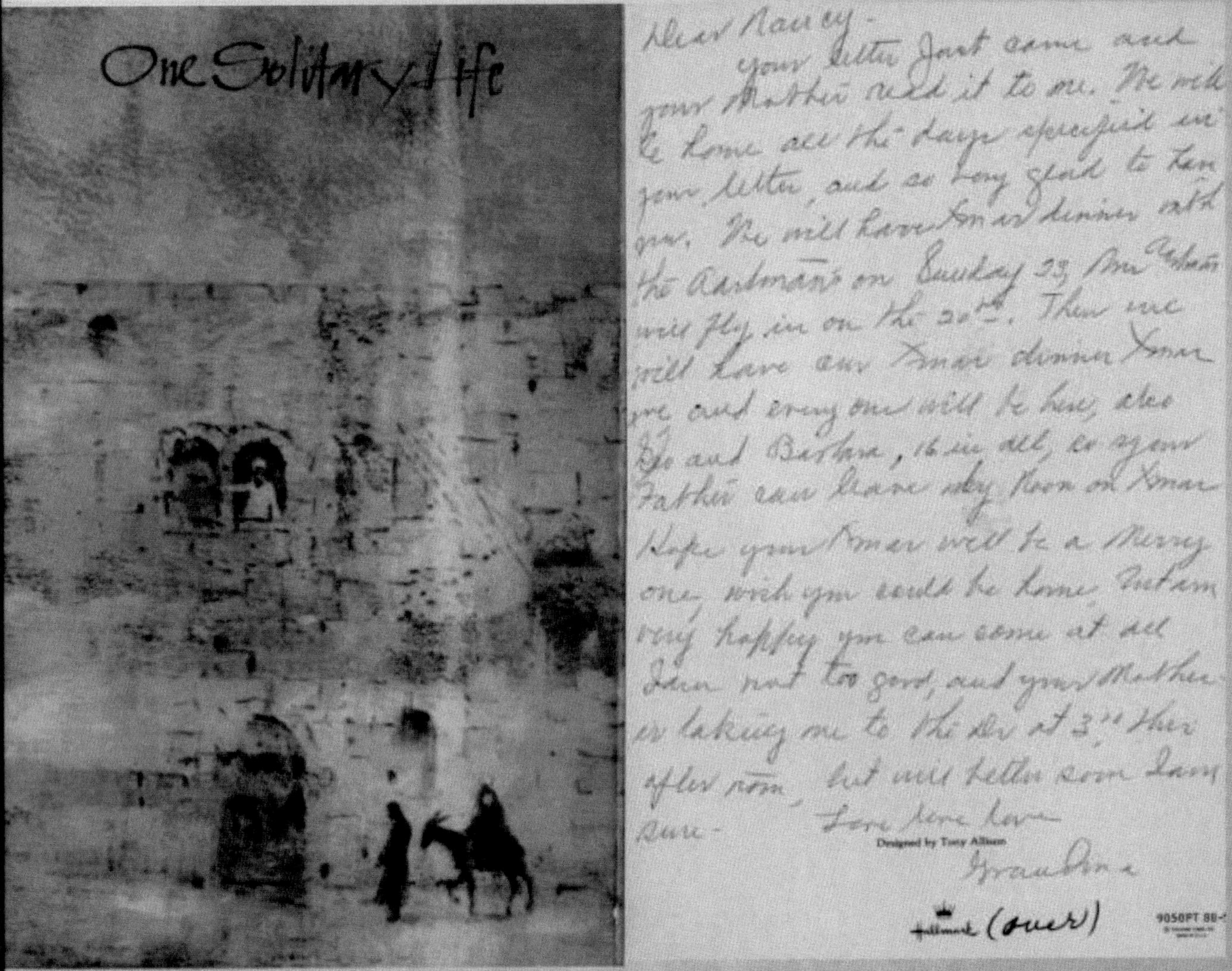
One Solitary Life

Dear Nancy,
Your letter just came and your Mother read it to me. We will be home all the days specified in your letter, and so very glad to have you. We will have dinner with the Aartmans on Sunday the 23rd. Mrs Aartman will fly in on the 20th. Then we will have our Christmas dinner on Christmas Eve and everyone will be here, also Geo and Bertha, 16 in all, so your Father can leave by noon on Christmas Day. Hope your Christmas will be a Merry one, wish you could be home. I am very happy you can come at all. I am not too good and your Mother is taking me to the Dr at 3:00 Thursday afternoon, but
I'll be better soon I am sure.

Love from your
Grandma

This Christmas Card from Nancy's Grandmother Mina was likely sent in the mid 1960's while Nancy was in college.

From Nancy's Nephew Jim:

There were many good times and things about Aunt Nancy. I remember when my grandfather offered to take her to Jerusalem to the holy land and she said she would rather go to Spain or Italy. It was a great laugh since she was a nun. They went to where she wanted to go.

Above: Nancy and Jim together at her celebration in 1987. Between ten and fifteen years later, she poses with Jim's son Aaron.

Below: A photo Nancy took of Aaron and Jim at a family gathering in the summer of 2015

Nancy with her sister Kathy and her nephew Tom

From Nancy's Niece Serena:

Every year, the day after Thanksgiving, the women in our family took a shopping trip to Saulsalito, California. We always went to Scoma's, this really nice seafood restaurant. Nancy's favorite thing was to prank our server. She would go into a joke store during the day to find the perfect thing, like a fake ice cube with bugs in it, then she'd show it to the waiter and absolutely crack up at their reaction. One year in particular stands out in my memory. She got a wind-up cockroach that would skitter across the table. She went to such lengths to plan it, she even bought a newspaper just so she could keep the thing hidden until the perfect moment. Once she let it go, she couldn't stop laughing the whole meal.

We would break off in groups to go shopping and meet up at the end of the day. I was with Nancy and she took me to FAO Schwartz, the Toy Store. I don't remember what I bought but she called me a "real good bargain shopper." She was so proud of that she bragged about my shopping to all the other women at the table.

peace cannot be kept by force.
it can only be achieved
by understanding.

Albert Einstein

every blade of grass has its angel that bends over it and whispers, "grow, grow."

The Talmud

bagnaio and Villa Lante

rt is one of those things we simply must do so that our

spirit may continue to grow.

this day is too dear with its hopes and invitations to waste a moment on yesterday. Ralph Waldo Emerson

he who is fixed to a star does not change his mind.

Leonardo da Vinci

The Windows of my soul
I throw wide open to the sun.

John Greenlief

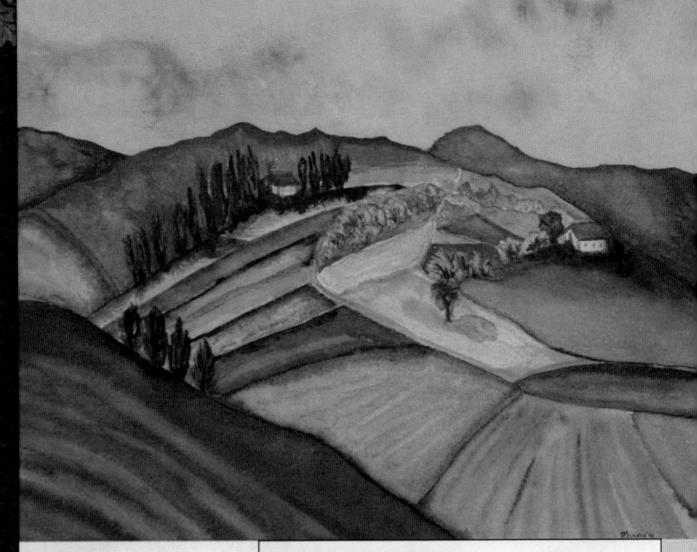

And the verse falls to the soul like dew to the pasture.

Work of sight is done. now do heartwork on the pictures within you.

Rainer Maria Rilke

There are always flowers *for those* who want to see them.
Henri Matisse

There are two ways to live your life.
One is as though nothing is a miracle.
The other is as if everything is a miracle.
Albert Einstein

Not knowing when the dawn will come, I open every door.
Emily Dickson

SISTER NANCY MUNRO

if your pictures aren't good enough, you aren't close enough.

Robert Capa

i found i could say things with colors and shapes that i couldn't say any other way - things i had no words for.

Georgia O'keefe

the camera is my tool. through it
i give reason to everything around me.

Andre Kertesz

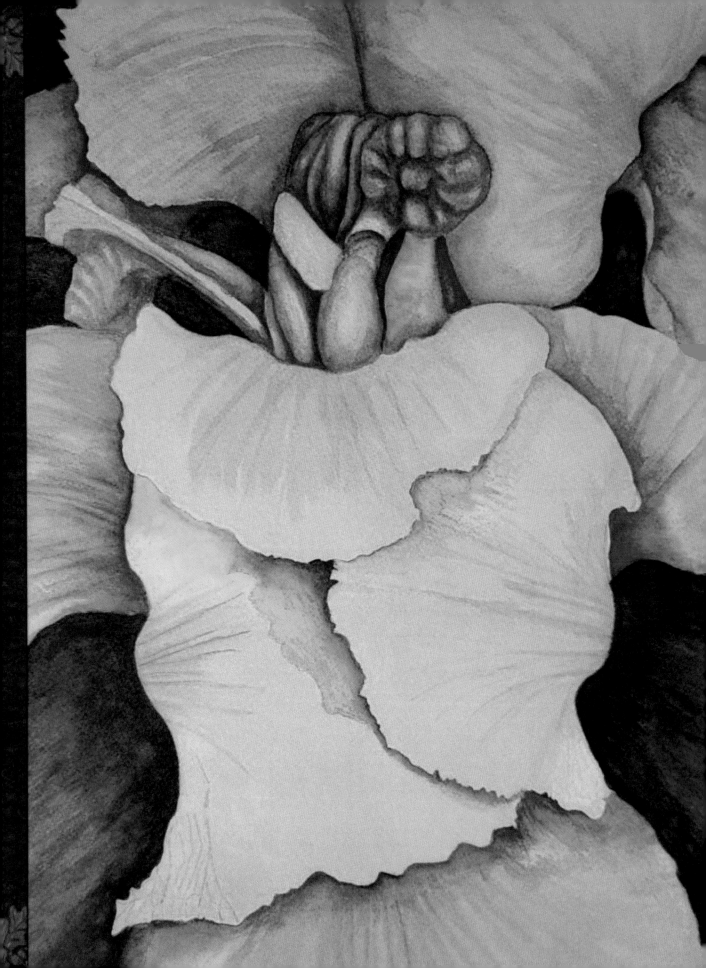

You don't have to be tall to see the moon. *African Proverb*

Made in the USA
Las Vegas, NV
16 November 2023

80934903R00062